All Families

Grandparent Families

by Connor Stratton

www.focusreaders.com

Copyright © 2025 by Focus Readers®, Mendota Heights, MN 55120. All rights reserved. No part of this book may be reproduced or utilized in any form or by any means without written permission from the publisher.

Focus Readers is distributed by North Star Editions:
sales@northstareditions.com | 888-417-0195

Produced for Focus Readers by Red Line Editorial.

Photographs ©: iStockphoto, cover, 1; Shutterstock Images, 4, 6, 8, 11, 13, 14–15, 16, 18, 21, 22, 24, 27, 29

Library of Congress Cataloging-in-Publication Data
Names: Stratton, Connor, author.
Title: Grandparent families / by Connor Stratton.
Description: Mendota Heights, MN: Focus Readers, [2025] | Series: All families | Includes bibliographical references and index. | Audience: Grades 2-3
Identifiers: LCCN 2024022335 (print) | LCCN 2024022336 (ebook) | ISBN 9798889983903 (hardcover) | ISBN 9798889984184 (paperback) | ISBN 9798889984733 (pdf) | ISBN 9798889984467 (ebook)
Subjects: LCSH: Grandparents as parents--Juvenile literature. | Grandparent and child--Juvenile literature. | Families--Juvenile literature.
Classification: LCC HQ759.9 .S757 2025 (print) | LCC HQ759.9 (ebook) | DDC 306.87/45--dc23/eng/20240716
LC record available at https://lccn.loc.gov/2024022335
LC ebook record available at https://lccn.loc.gov/2024022336

Printed in the United States of America
Mankato, MN
012025

About the Author

Connor Stratton writes and edits nonfiction children's books. He lives in Minnesota.

Table of Contents

CHAPTER 1
Nights with Grandma 5

CHAPTER 2
Grandfamilies 9

Race and Grandfamilies 14

CHAPTER 3
Challenges and Strengths 17

CHAPTER 4
Full of Feelings 23

Focus on Grandparent Families • 28
Glossary • 30
To Learn More • 31
Index • 32

Chapter 1

Nights with Grandma

A boy has homework to do. But the **pharmacy** closes soon. His grandmother needs to refill her medicine. She does not speak much English. So, the boy calls the pharmacy. He orders the refill.

 Grandparents sometimes need to take lots of pills to stay healthy.

 Children and grandparents can both learn things from each other.

Then, the boy and his grandma do homework. He uses the school's tablet. She helps him learn division.

Before bed, the grandmother tells stories. She talks about when she was a child. The boy learns about the big family she grew up with. The boy listens closely. He feels he's a part of that family.

The boy gets sad when he thinks of his mother. He misses her. But he loves his grandma. And he knows she loves him back.

Did You Know?

In the United States, more than two million children are being raised by their grandparents.

Chapter 2

Grandfamilies

Grandparent families are sometimes called grandfamilies. In these families, grandparents are the main caregivers. Caregivers help kids stay safe and healthy. They provide food and clothing.

Caregivers make sure kids are loved, and they help guide kids' behavior.

Caregivers teach kids about the world, too.

Grandfamilies can include **multigenerational** homes. That means the parents also live there. The grandparents may share childcare with the parents. In other grandfamilies, it's just the grandparents and grandchildren.

Parents love their children. And they want to be able to take care of their kids. But it's not always possible. Sometimes, parents die

 About 1 in every 12 children is part of a grandfamily.

when their kids are still young. Other times, parents have to leave. They may be sent to prison. Or they may be forced to leave the country. Other times, parents aren't doing their job to care for their kids.

Government workers might decide these parents shouldn't raise their children anymore.

Sometimes parents are there **physically**. But they can't provide care. For example, parents may struggle with **addiction**. That can make it hard to raise kids.

Did You Know?

About 1 percent of US children are Indigenous. But 8 percent of children in grandfamilies are Indigenous.

 It's okay to feel sad when a parent is struggling.

Many grandparents step in during these situations. Sometimes grandfamilies last until the kids become adults. Other times, parents just need a few months or years. Then they can become the main caregivers again.

MANY IDENTITIES

Race and Grandfamilies

The **criminal justice system** can have large impacts on families. This system is often unfair. **Racism** is common. For example, using certain drugs is against the law. White people and Black people use drugs at similar rates. But more Black people are put in prison for it.

As a result, the system takes more Black parents away from their families. This leads to more Black children in grandfamilies. Black children make up 14 percent of all American children. But 25 percent of children in grandfamilies are Black.

Many grandfamilies form when a parent is in prison.

Chapter 3

Challenges and Strengths

Grandparent families can face a variety of challenges. These challenges are often linked with how the grandfamily formed. The reasons can be very painful. One example is the loss of a parent.

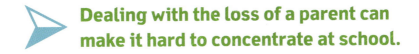
Dealing with the loss of a parent can make it hard to concentrate at school.

 Starting at a new school can lead to sadness and loneliness.

This loss affects both grandparents and grandchildren.

Also, grandfamilies may form suddenly. This quick change can be difficult. Kids often have to live in a new place. So, moving can mean leaving friends. It can also disrupt routines. Kids need time to adjust to these changes.

Money can be another challenge. A family may have depended on a parent's income. This money paid for food, transportation, and clothing. Losing that income can be hard. The grandfamily may not be able to meet basic needs.

Age differences can be another struggle. Things change over time.

Children face new issues, such as social media. Grandparents did not have to deal with these issues when they were young. That can make it harder for grandfamilies to connect.

Even so, grandfamilies have many strengths. Grandparents can pass on **culture** to their grandkids. Also,

Did You Know?

Differences between kids and grandparents sometimes involve new technology.

 Cooking is one way for grandparents to share their culture with grandkids.

grandparents have been through a lot. They've learned how to handle life's challenges. Grandchildren can learn from this resilience.

Chapter 4

Full of Feelings

Roles in grandfamilies can be confusing. Grandparents take on the role of parents. Kids may not like them taking the parents' place. Roles can be extra confusing when the parents are still there.

Sometimes confusion leads to anger. Talking about it can often help.

23

 Kids and grandparents can help each other deal with grief.

The parents may seem more like siblings. But children often remember how things were before the grandfamily formed. They might

24

want to connect with their parents in the old way. Not being able to do that can be hard.

Being raised by grandparents can lead to strong feelings. If parents died or left, **grief** is very common. Children may also feel angry. These emotions are hard to deal with. But they are normal. And they are okay.

Processing strong feelings is important. Communicating can help. Children can talk to adults they trust. Kids can write about it.

They can also draw or act out their feelings. Sometimes, adults can find ways to help. Other times, feeling understood is enough.

Children in grandfamilies may feel different from other kids. For example, some parents play sports with their kids. Grandparents might not be able to play sports.

Did You Know?

Aunts or uncles can be good adults to talk to. School **counselors** can help, too.

 All families are different, and that's okay.

Feeling different can be painful. But everyone is different in their own way. Kids can be kind. This helps people feel less alone. It also helps them heal.

FOCUS ON
Grandparent Families

Write your answers on a separate piece of paper.

1. Summarize the main ideas of Chapter 2.

2. What issues do you have to deal with that your grandparents did not?

3. In the United States, how many grandparents are raising their grandchildren?
    - A. fewer than 200,000
    - B. more than two million
    - C. nearly 200 million

4. Why can a grandfamily have challenges in the beginning?
    - A. The family forms because of a sudden change.
    - B. The family has more money than it needs.
    - C. The people in the family aren't related to one another.

5. What does **resilience** mean in this book?

*Also, grandparents have been through a lot. They've learned how to handle life's challenges. Grandchildren can learn from this **resilience**.*

    A. a way of teaching older people new ideas
    B. the ability to get through hard times
    C. having children taking care of parents

6. What does **communicating** mean in this book?

Communicating *can help. Children can talk to adults they trust.*

    A. growing up with a new family
    B. talking to another person
    C. learning quickly

Answer key on page 32.

Glossary

addiction
A need to keep doing something. An addiction may involve drugs or alcohol.

counselors
People whose job is to listen and to help people work through problems.

criminal justice system
The system of rules, processes, and agencies that deal with crime and enforce an area's laws.

culture
A group of people and how they live, such as customs and beliefs.

grief
A feeling of deep sadness or pain over a loss.

multigenerational
Having children, parents, and grandparents together.

pharmacy
A place that sells medicine.

physically
In a way that has to do with the body.

racism
Hatred or mistreatment of people because of their skin color or ethnicity.

To Learn More

BOOKS

Kentner, Julie. *Immigrant and Refugee Families*. Mendota Heights, MN: Focus Readers, 2023.

Polin, C. J. *My Family*. Buffalo, NY: Rosen Publishing, 2023.

Schuh, Mari C. *My Life with a Grandparent with Alzheimer's Disease*. Mankato, MN: Amicus, 2024.

NOTE TO EDUCATORS

Visit **www.focusreaders.com** to find lesson plans, activities, links, and other resources related to this title.

Index

A
addiction, 12
age differences, 19–20

B
Black children, 14

C
caregivers, 9–10, 13
communicating, 25–26
criminal justice system, 14
culture, 20

D
death of a parent, 7, 10–11, 17–18, 25
drugs, 14

F
friends, 19

G
grief, 25

H
homework, 5–6

I
Indigenous children, 12

M
money, 19
multigenerational homes, 10

P
prison, 11, 14

R
racism, 14
routines, 19

Answer Key: 1. Answers will vary; 2. Answers will vary; 3. B; 4. A; 5. B; 6. B